Too Emotional

Ruth Cena

BookLeaf Publishing

Presentation by *BookLeaf Publishing*

Web: www.bookleafpub.com

E-mail: info@bookleafpub.com

ISBN: 9789358312393

First edition 2023

For anyone who has ever been told: "you're too emotional". To be without emotion is to be without passion, and I would rather be nothing than to be passionless.

ACKNOWLEDGEMENT

I couldn't have made this collection happen
without the inspiration of my sister Candi
Bartlett. You have single handedly inspired me
to be a better human and to continue to chase my
dreams. I hope you feel this collection is a love
letter to everything you have taught me and
helped me see.
To BookLeaf Publishing for the opportunity to
take the first step in pursuing my dreams.

PREFACE

Too Emotional is my first professional work, and is my heart on paper. I've often been branded too emotional, and used to resent that. Now, I embrace it, letting it push me forward in life and art. This collection of poetry is a shifting perspective of life, thoughts and the emotions that color our every day. It is my hope that everyone feels themselves in this collection.

Caves

Caves are an empty thing.
Most are nothing but air and dirt.
They hold nothing of value.
But if I am a cave empty and vast,
Does that make me empty too?
Would I crumble under the weight of my own
expectations?
Caves are an empty thing. They hold nothing of
value.
If I am a cave, am I valueless too?
If I were to crumble, would a little bit of you
shatter?
If even ever so slightly.
Or would you be clueless to my faltering?
Caves are an empty thing. Valueless and
crumbling.
If I am a cave, who would explore my broken
parts?
Is anyone brave enough to endure my
emptiness?
Who could plant in a barren land and believe it
will bear fruit?
For I am an empty thing.
And no one could love an empty thing.

Power in Me

I grow as a tree around an electrical wire.
Those things that cut through me, can not
destroy me.
I may no longer be whole, but there is still
beauty here.
Though it is not the same, I find peace in my
missing parts.

I am not electric, but there is power in me.
Unassuming and stoic,
I push past those that test me and grow in spite
of their efforts.
I am a tree that grows around the electric wire.
Fighting the odds and defying logic.
Watch me take on any pain and I will come back
bearing leaves.

I am not electric, but I am strong.
Obstacles that try to hold me down only fuel me.
Stare at me as you would at a broken glass,
saddened by the cracks, but fearful of being cut.
Confused on how one can be fragile yet
dangerous.

I am not electric, but I am unstoppable.

Every storm that knocks down my branches,
can never stop me from growing them back.
Where the damage was once done,
only beauty will be seen.
For as a tree growing around an electric wire, I
will persevere.

Feel Shiny

For as long as I remember, I have been a dull,
gray stone.
Smooth on one side, rough on the other.
I have stayed and been washed over countless
times.
Letting the waves shape me, change me.
Becoming less of what I was and more of who it
made me.
But my other side left untouched,
Became rougher as time passed, so it seems.
What if it isn't rough at all?
Just the contrast of the nothingness that has
become the norm.
What if texture is the thing that makes us more
than a stone?
More than a withering thing being crushed,
shaped and changed by the waves.
Smooth is not what I wished to be, but the
outcome of a forced situation.
The grooves and marks I wear show my past.
Why should I polish them just to feel shiny?
I should have pride in my wear as it shows I
have lived.
Be free in myself and my unchangeable parts.

Even if I am but a dull gray thing, I choose to
sparkle.
For even a gray rock deserves to feel shiny.

Moments

Moments
Fleeting, precious seconds ticking
The most valuable slipping by unnoticed
Not until time has passed
Making you wish you had seen the beauty in the
moment
In the moment
Seems like a simple way to live
Yet our days slip into meaningless arguments
Lost moments when fighting takes place
Where we live in silence
Lost moments
Regret, filling when we let bad overrule good
Negative emotions are suffocating
Overbearing
Making me feel lost in time
I hope for clarity to separate my hate for me
For the love we have together
Live in the moments we share
Shared moments
Basking in the warmth of your smile
Smiling for no particular reason
Your fingers laced through mine
Time is fleeting
But if we allow it them

Moments can last forever
I choose to live in moments
For the moments are what write our stories

Find Myself

I promise one day I will find myself.
Hidden in the sand.
Crying for all the broken things
that I could never mend.
Holding hope out for the world to change.
But knowing that it won't.
It's no wonder why I hide away,
instead of showing my soul.

I promise I will find myself.
One day it's bound to be.
Laying on a frozen bed
waiting to be freed.
Bound to all the madness
that has tied me by this rope.
Surviving very nearly
by the legs of golden hope.

I promise one day I will find me.
Floating to the shore.
Wounds will be healing nicely,
scars replace the sores.
Water will drown my sadness
as I bounce and go along.

Nothing is easy but I'm trying
Which is more than I could say before.

I promise I will find me someday
Smiling with all my might.
I'll feel joy within my deepest thoughts
and love within my light.
I'll let past guilt melt away,
but hope the lesson learned will stay.
I feel I'm closer than ever before,
to spread my wings and finally soar.

Unfinished

Why was I cursed with this manner
of wanting to do so much but stopping
In the middle, always unfinished
How could one dream so big
Think so much, only to sit and stare
Cursed to never have the drive to complete
But to always have the want to start new things
Everything is always left unfinished
Am I missing pieces
A broken thing, doomed to be incomplete
forever
No amount of glue can make a cracked cup
usable
How do I save myself from drowning
When there are no waves holding me down
Why is every dream so strong at first, then
fizzles away like chalk in the rain.
So beautiful, yet so easily washed away
Every thought left unfinished
Every project, and new hope alike.
I sit here and I stare forever more.
Not knowing what can shake me from this
stillness.
From this delusion that I cannot finish what I've
started.

What will it take for me to snap myself out of
this habit I have allowed to consume me.
When will I finally see that I alone have built the
wall that stands in front of me blocking me from
doing what I need to.
I am the hand pushing me down, holding me in
this same place.
I am the one breaking my pencil tips, so that
every sentence I start is left unfinished.
It is not the lack of want that is holding me back.
Instead it is the lack of force pushing me
forward.
With nothing to lose, there is nothing to
motivate me to gain.
Except that simple fact, that I know I need to.
I need to finish what I started
How do I turn this colorless portrait into art?
How do I learn to complete what I have always
left
Unfinished..

Fine Line

Everyday, I walk a fine line.
Tiptoeing past the things that haunt my delicate
mind.
If I linger too long, I will be consumed by the
uncertainty.
But if I move too fast, I could be destroyed by
the absurdity.
For if you stare at a painting too long, the
meaning will change.
Museum walls crumble with the falsities that
haunt them.
I too have become something I wasn't before.

Everyday I walk a fine line.
I am colorless masquerading as a rainbow.
A happy portrait painted by undying sadness.
Weeds dressed up in bright colors, only beautiful
for a brief moment.
Where a smile hangs, pain swims in the
background.
How can you create a bright picture with black
and white paint?
Look closely at my porcelain smile and you'll
see it's painted on.

Everyday I walk a fine line.
A balancing act between being okay and falling
apart.
A happy face is always there, but so much
lingers under the surface.
Each day is a new challenge but no one sees me
struggle.
You can't pity what you don't know is breaking.
So I teeter between two worlds with grace and
agony.
Look at me in awe for you don't see what weighs
me down.

Everyday I walk a fine line.
I hover over the depths of the earth.
Trying not to fall into the unknown.
Holding on hope that my line will not snap,
even when it bends and quivers beneath the
weight of expectations.
Will I ever hold my breath long enough to live in
the silence?
Or will I forever be cursed to walk a fine line?

Fire

What if all this time I've been a fire in hiding?
Claiming victim at the forests I've burned down.
Lighting matches in my path and turning away,
Refusing to feel the heat from my own blaze.
Relentlessly destroying all that is good.
Without blinking an eye, hidden even from
myself in disguise.
Always felt like someone was chasing me.
Dousing me with gasoline as I cried out for help.
All along I held the matches in my palm,
striking them along my jaw.

What if I am a silent hurricane?
Destroying the land you didn't know you had,
As I shook your hand with a smile on my face.
Could I break your home, without even
knowing.
Holding a sledgehammer, where flowers should
be.
Wrecking your dreams, while I hold you
screaming why.

What if I could write a million stories where I
was the martyr and never once tell a lie?
Can you be the secret villain in your own story?

Danger always found me, that's the way I told it.
What if all this time, it was me that would call it
to me?
Taunt it to engage me, take me out and let it
break me,
Fall back on the floor, crying out for someone
else to fix it for me.
Keeping the readers engaged, but far enough
away they never see me for who I really am.

What if I have never seen my reflection, looking
only in a broken mirror.
It's easier to ignore what you cannot see.
Stay blind to the knife I am driving in my own
heart.
Outside it is a fairy-tale,
But what if there is no happy ending here?
I cannot drink from the well I have poisoned
without getting sick.

Natural Disaster

Hey look at me, I'm a natural disaster.
Dress like a princess, bite like a raptor.
No one sees me coming with my pretty little
face.
Whiskey and acid, covered in lace.
I'll poison the cup you're drinking from,
while holding your hand as we dance in the sun.
You believe me as I tell you, all the things I've
said before.
Don't forget to check my back, crossed fingers
are hard to ignore.

I'm a natural disaster baby.
To love me is to admit you're crazy.
Only a hurricane can wear its red flags
out in the open like designer bags;
And no one bats an eye,
as destruction blows by.
You can't say you hadn't been warned.
If you stay in my path, you're bound to be
scorned.
But neither of us will admit that I destroyed this.
We continue to walk with ignorant bliss.

I am a natural Disaster, love.

I will forever rain down sorrow from above.
But even after the darkest storm,
Flowers grow back, and beauty forms.
Lightness moves in and replaces the black,
helping us forget everything destroyed in its
path.
A garden grows where there once was debris,
beauty and forgiveness washing me clean.

See You're Beautiful

You hold your head high and wear your smile
convincingly.
People who don't know you believe you.
They look into your sparkling eyes and see
nothing but joy.
Standing alone as your guard drops down I
know you're hurting.
Each expectation you have clouds you and you
just want to drown them.
You look up and your eyes still sparkle, but I can
see the truth there.
I feel the burning you have for yourself.
Your cold heart aches to feel something other
than regret.
I wish I could make you see you're beautiful.
The way your laughter fills a room and changes
moods.
You're more than the dark sea you drown
yourself in.
You're bigger than the past that haunts you.
I could hold a mirror to your shining face,
and I know you would refuse to see what I see.
You would rather take the blame than admit you
deserve better.
I wish you could see you're beautiful.

Lazy Sunday

I live for our lazy Sundays
The days where we stay in bed with curtains
open
Smiling as the sun pours in,
while we hide away from the world
Not always in conversation but sharing just the
same space.
For even on a lazy Sunday, you always make me
feel seen..

I breathe for our unspoken words
The small glances that convey an entire
conversation
Your eyes surging into mine filling me up with
exactly what I was looking for
The moments where silence fills the whole room
in the best way
For even when unspoken, you always know the
right thing to say.

I search for the forgotten memories.
The days that slip by and have no meaning until
we miss them.
The moments that seem arbitrary but fill our
story with life and meaning,

For even the forgettable is memorable with you.

I cherish the warm breeze of summer days
When you lay with the sun on your face.
The days we let the warm breeze lull us to sleep,
For the slow, patient days with you is a living
dream.

Bouquet of Life

All the days we have lived together, are the roses
in this bouquet.
Red for the ones that are full of passion.
White for the patient moments between me and
you.
Yellow for the days that feel impossible, yet
somehow the beauty shines through.
Baby's-breathe for the secret moments in life.
The stolen glances when you don't think I notice
you looking at me
The whispers we share in the morning.
The lilies, both bloomed and buds, are the
dreams we hold.
The ones who have come to pass, those are the
bright large flowers adding the pop of color and
surprise.
Promises of the future, the things we have yet to
create; those are the buds that are shut tight but
hold promises of beauty.
Carnations are the whimsy, fun and unassuming.
They remind us that even the simple can be
beautiful.
The things we least expect to bring us joy and
beauty, often do.

The greenery is the consistency every bouquet
needs.
Bright, yet understated, happy yet balanced.
It's the routine, the basic everyday things that
keep us balanced.
Each flower is its own unique blend of beauty
and purpose.
Yet somehow they all fit together to make the
most beautiful bouquet of life.

Go Ahead

Life isn't easy.
Nothing of the sort.
It also isn't very long,
In fact it's really short.
When you're young,
it seems so vast.
As years go by,
you see it move so fast.
So heed my words,
go fly with the birds.
Chase your dreams,
wear your favorite jeans.
Dance in the rain,
sing through the pain.
Remember the good times,
and every hill you had to climb.
The bad moments too,
even when forgetting is all you want to do.
Love on the hard days,
spin in the sun's rays.
Look onto your past with a smile,
but never hold your missteps in exile.
Embrace your mistakes,
grieve the heartbreaks.
Laugh at the bad jokes,

believe in yourself when you feel broken.
Stand your ground,
scream when they say don't make a sound.
Keep your head high,
never feel guilty for asking, why?
Always remember you're loved.
Go ahead, and never give up.

Can We

Was this ever enough?
This bloom that we held so dearly,
keeping it so close to the vest that we nearly
crushed the life from it.
Can we build our whole landscape on one single
flower?
Do we forget the storms that destroyed the trees,
and only focus on the green we see?
Can we paint over the destruction that happened
here?
Even though we know you can't cover up a hole
with color.
The gaping blackness will always lay just
beneath.
Can we save this crumbling wall with one single
brick?
Ignoring the foundation that has been crumbling
for years,
building on top hoping it doesn't falter.
Can we pretend that we have a garden with a
single bloom?
Will we see the emptiness when we open our
eyes?
If we keep them closed tight, maybe we won't
see the truth.

We can live in our land of delusion and hope.
Build on our falling towers and dream that we
will never fall.

Rage

Rage.
A sweeping fire, burning through your chest.
Rising up to your throat,
radiating from your cheeks.
Pushing at your body with its might,
trying to break out and burn down everything
around you.
You can try to dampen the blaze,
smother the flames and hide the smoke.
But you know there is no hiding what is so
easily seen.
You cannot tame a wild fire.
And what is rage but a wild fire of the heart.
No one builds to rage,
Ii is an instant emotion that acts without thought.
It needs no fuel to spread and consume,
to engulf its hosts in the white hot flash of anger.
When the match is lit, it burns strong and bright.
When it reaches your eyes, they turn dark and
blank.
Consumed by the intensity that is buried in its
plague.
When it takes over, you feel as though you could
burst through your skin.

Anger seethes through you, embedding itself
deeper into you,
until you feel it pulsing through your blood.
Electricity and fire coursing through your veins.
How do you break free from the venom as it
chooses you?
Can you run from the inevitable, or should you
let it swallow you?
Giving into the war erupting within.

Passion

I was told once that I was too passionate.
I care too much for my own good.
That no one person should feel that deeply for
things that do not impact them.
The world's issues are not your issues.
As if I am to turn off the rage that flows through
me when I see injustice.
The fire that bubbles and burns when I continue
to watch the world crumble.
Passion is not a choice, but a responsibility.
It can be a weapon or a tool, depending on who
is wielding it.
Baseless, fact-less, uneducated facts make for
dangerous fuel,
stoking fires of ignorance.
Passion should not be felt for yourself alone.
Empathy, hope, truth should evoke passion for
others.
Injustice does not need to affect me to hurt me.
Fueled by the instances of hopelessness you
cannot change.
It is the white hot flash that burns when you see
another human treated like nothing.
It's the tears that can't be wiped away when we
watch our world go backwards.

Anger rises from the bold hypocrisies that replay daily.

The false narratives that damage the truth and endanger our most vulnerable.

Passion is the product of my restlessness, my desperation for change.

You say it doesn't affect me and I say it affects us all.

We all deserve the greatness promised.

America the Broken

Are you one of the privileged
Made to believe you are owed everything
Each and every promise fulfilled by your desire
to be rewarded
Regardless of the backs that are stepped on to
get where you are
Indirectly the product of all that tramples on the
forgotten
Cease to pardon your actions and take note of
your blindness
Avoiding the truth does not save you from
responsibility
Teach to love all but vote for those who hate
those who are different
Hatred spreads like wildfires through the lies
Everyone is to blame
Belittling our intelligence with false facts,
exploiting ignorance and hate
Rally for your rights but spit on those whose
rights are actually being taken
Oblivious to the agenda being pushed out
Knives in the hearts of those who have bled for
this country
Every person deserves the American dream
No matter what your beliefs say

Be

Be pretty,
but don't care what people think about you.
Be thin,
but don't be too skinny.
Don't let them take you for granted,
but never speak your mind out of turn.
Be independent,
but know your place around a man.
Be honest,
but respect other people's opinions.
Stand your ground,
but don't overstep your place.
Be loyal,
but love those who hurt you unconditionally.
Be vigilant,
but don't think that everyone is out to get you.
Speak up,
but don't be too emotional.
Be your own person,
but don't be too different.
Be caring,
but mind your business.

Do it all,

but don't spread yourself too thin.
Be clever,
but don't show off.
Be confident,
but dress respectfully.
Work hard,
but put your family first.
Be brave,
but remember you're just a girl.
Be a woman,
but only the way we want you to be.
We say, it is time to be done listening to what
they want us to be.
Reject the ever-changing expectations of what a
woman is,
and just be.

We are all Women

We are all women.
Can you hear us scream as another one dies?
As your laws rule our bodies, we watch our
sisters fall away.
You can say what you want to sell your agenda.
We are not blind or accepting your false truths.
We are all women.
We know when you say it's for us, you mean it's
for your control over us.
Our grandmothers are tired from fighting this
fight.
They thought they won, and then you ripped
their victory from under us all.
What once felt like normal human rights, now
feels like war.
Haven't we been here before?
Why would we go back to the past?
We are all women.
I am safe here in my state but I see my sisters
who are being failed.
Ones who didn't choose their fate but have to
deal with the repercussions.
Ones who were taken advantage of, too young to
become a mother.

Ones who wanted deeply to love this baby, but
the universe had other plans.
But you make her keep it in her, just to remind
her of how she failed.
Making her a living grave, and for what?
To prove to her that you never found value in her
for her,
but only for her ability to create life?
And when her body says no, then what?
She is left to deal with the pain and the physical
reminders of what can't be.
We are all women.
Those who have been left to feel abandoned and
scared.
The ones who are unheard by those who say
they represent them.
You do not represent us as you rip away our
right to choose.
Our right to have a say in our own future.
When you tell one woman she doesn't have a
right, you tell us all.
We are all women.
The girls who will be women one day, who don't
yet know how you have betrayed them.
We cry for the uncertainty of their futures.
For the lack of ability to tell them it will be okay
and mean it with certainty.

How could you look at your daughter and tell
her that she doesn't have a voice when it comes
to her own body?
Your state dictates how you can live and be.
That you have to carefully think about what
state, town, county you live in.
Because one day it could most certainly mean
life or death.
We are all women.
The ones who have had their innocence taken
and are made to feel ashamed.
Asked what were you wearing, instead of how
could this happen.
The ones who are shamed for loving themselves
because we are too tempting for the other sex.
When we will teach men to respect women,
instead of teaching women to fear men.
We are all women.
The ones who have been left alone, told to wait
until they are close to death.
The ones who hear, sorry there is nothing we can
do.
The ones who have to bear the constant
reminders of what they lost.
We are all women, and together we stand.

One Day

One day
I dream we will have peace.
We can see brightness in the future.
All people will feel safe.
No one race will have the upper hand.
It won't be a crime to progress and grow away
from the past.
It won't seem treasonous to want control of your
own body.
One day
I see hope for the country.
Where young people will have a voice.
Where we can see the change helping all who
live here.
Where the color of your skin doesn't decide if
you are suspicious.
Where religion is a choice but your body is a
right.
One day
I hope the sides will be less divided.
That we can finally understand we just want all
humans to feel loved.
No matter how you feel about our life choices,
we still have a right to live.

Where the gender of a stranger didn't evoke
anger, but understanding.
One day
I want to feel compassion, regardless of your
political affiliation.
That people would no longer justify horrible
things by someone's past.
When someone is a victim, they aren't trying to
paint them as a villain.
Where right or left you can see that where we
are is broken.
One day
I hope for a world that is safe for my trans
friends.
Safe for every race.
Safe for every gender or lack thereof.
Safe for those to love who they want.
Safe for women to live without fear.
One day
I hope we are better.

Here lies

Here lies the person I used to be.
The person who was beaten and bruised into
silence.
The person who never truly loved herself,
so never felt the need to stick up for anyone else.
Here lies the girl who hid in shame.
The one who never spoke her own name.
Who hid from the guilt of man's choice.
Who lived in my shame when I had no voice.
Here lies all my past mistakes.
For I can no longer carry them on my back.
I deserve to free myself from their shackles.
Because everyone fails sometimes.
Here lies hiding behind grace.
I no longer care about who I offend.
If I think you're wrong I'll fight to the end.
For every human deserves a voice, and I will no
longer let mine stay silent.
Here lies my fear of being disliked.
Nothing matters if we are spitting in the face of
our neighbors.
I will stand for those who have no legs.
And fight for those who don't feel worth it.
I will see those who have been ignored.
Here lies all the excuses I have hidden behind.

I will stand with those who have been
marginalized.
I will be the megaphone for those whose voices
have been muted.
I will be the hope you need on a day when you
feel hopeless.
I will be there for those who have never met me.
Here lies all of my doubt.
I will push through the uncertainty.
I will help those who need saving.
And I promise,
I will never lie down and let you fall alone.
Here lies the patriarchy,
may it rest in pieces.